INTERIOR

DESIGN

COLORING
BOOK

**ROXANA
RAMOS**

LETTRA

Contributors:
Rosa Cueva
Melissa Fernandez
Gabriela Morales
Pamela Raygada

ISBN: 1523990538
ISBN-13: 978-1523990535

To all coloring fans,
paper lovers,
and artists by heart.

Kitchens

We recommend using warm
colors for a comfy look.

Color Scheme #1

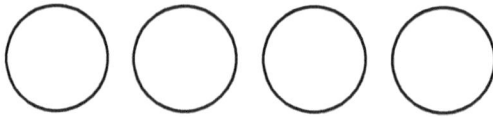

Color Scheme #2

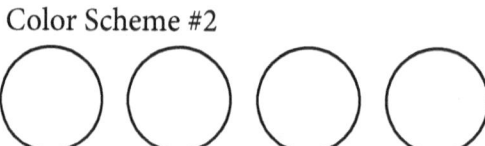

Color Scheme #3

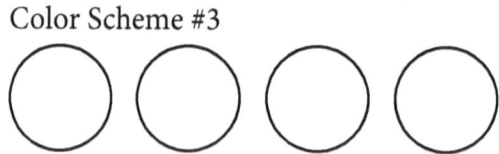

Color Scheme #1

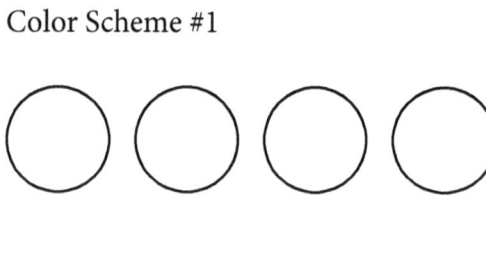

Color Scheme #2

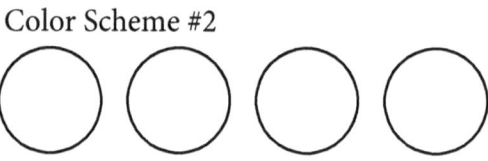

Color Scheme #3

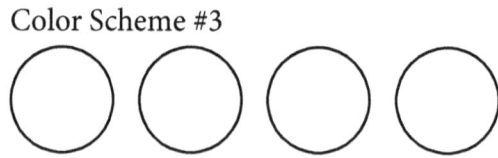

Color Scheme #1

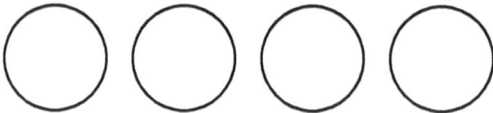

Color Scheme #2

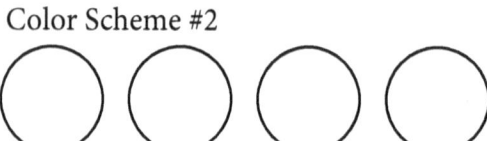

Color Scheme #3

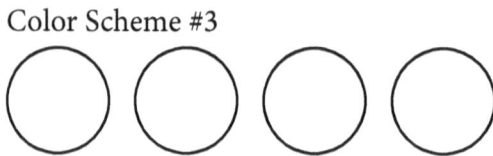

Living Rooms

We recommend using calm colors like
pastels for a relaxing environment.

Color Scheme #1

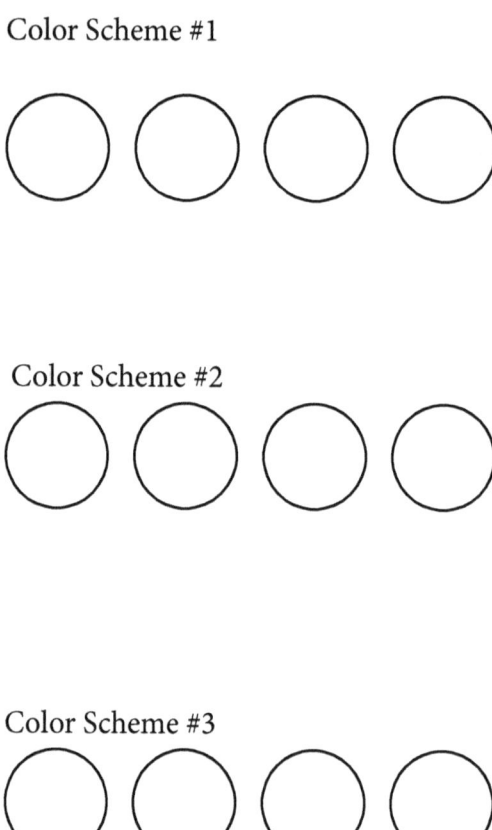

Color Scheme #2

Color Scheme #3

Color Scheme #1

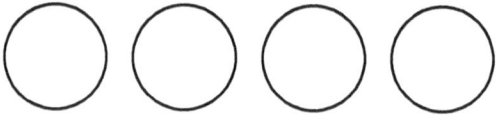

Color Scheme #2

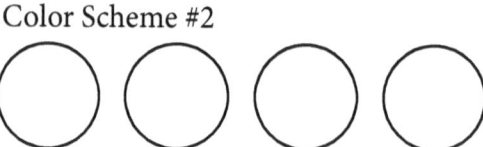

Color Scheme #3

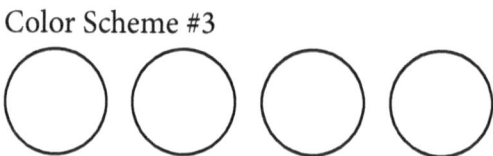

Color Scheme #1

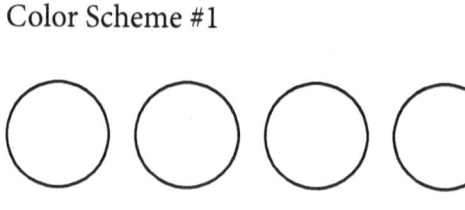

Color Scheme #2

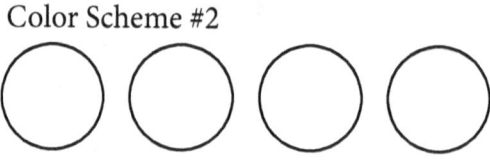

Color Scheme #3

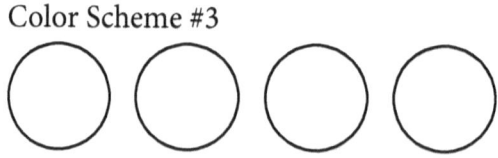

Color Scheme #1

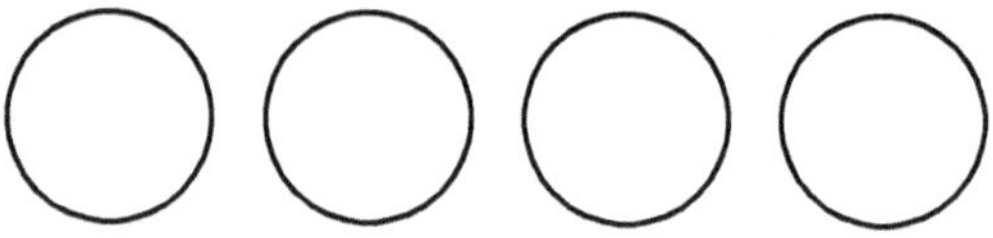

Color Scheme #2

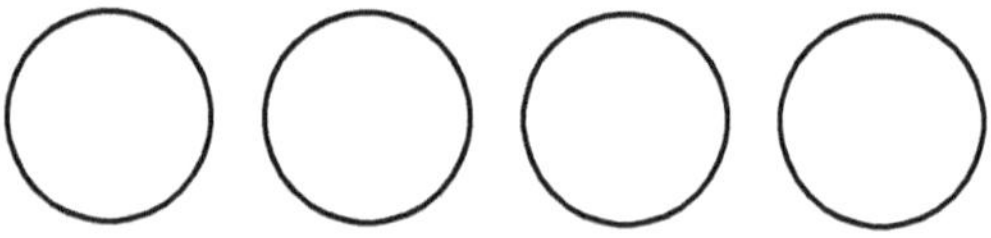

Color Scheme #3

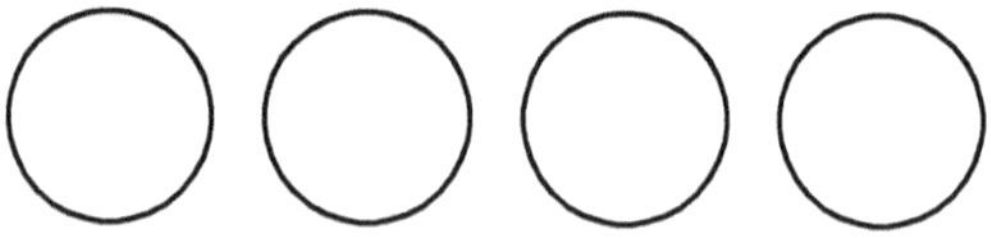

Color Scheme #1

Color Scheme #2

Color Scheme #3

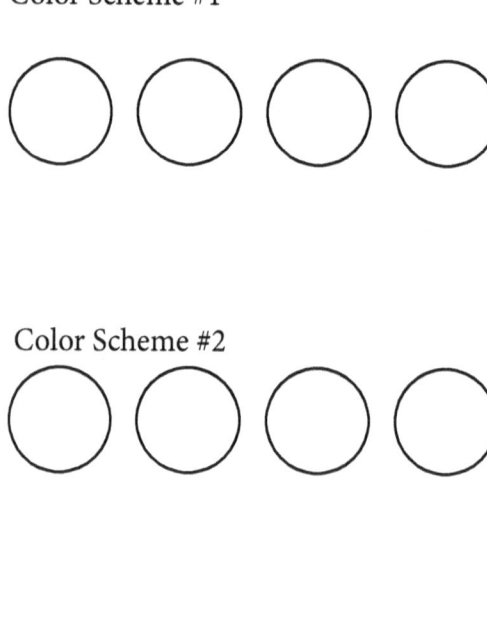

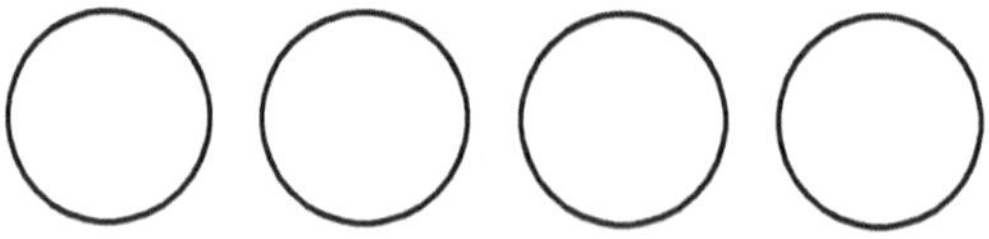

Color Scheme #1

Color Scheme #2

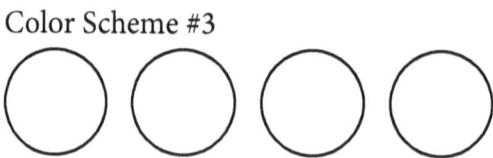

Color Scheme #3

Exteriors

Go outside and seek for inspiration.
Different times of day will give
you different types of shadows.

Color Scheme #1

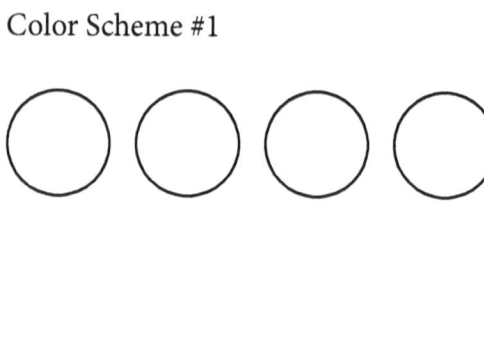

Color Scheme #2

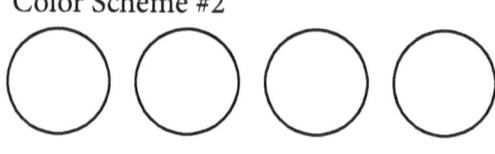

Color Scheme #3

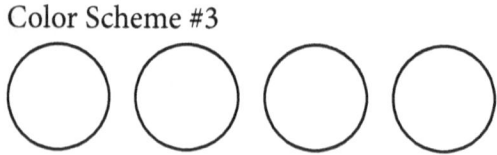

Color Scheme #1

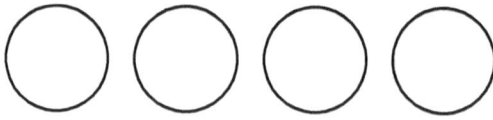

Color Scheme #2

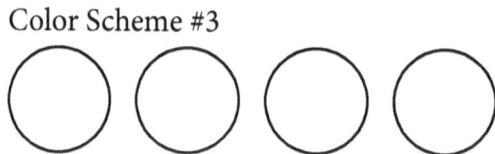

Color Scheme #3

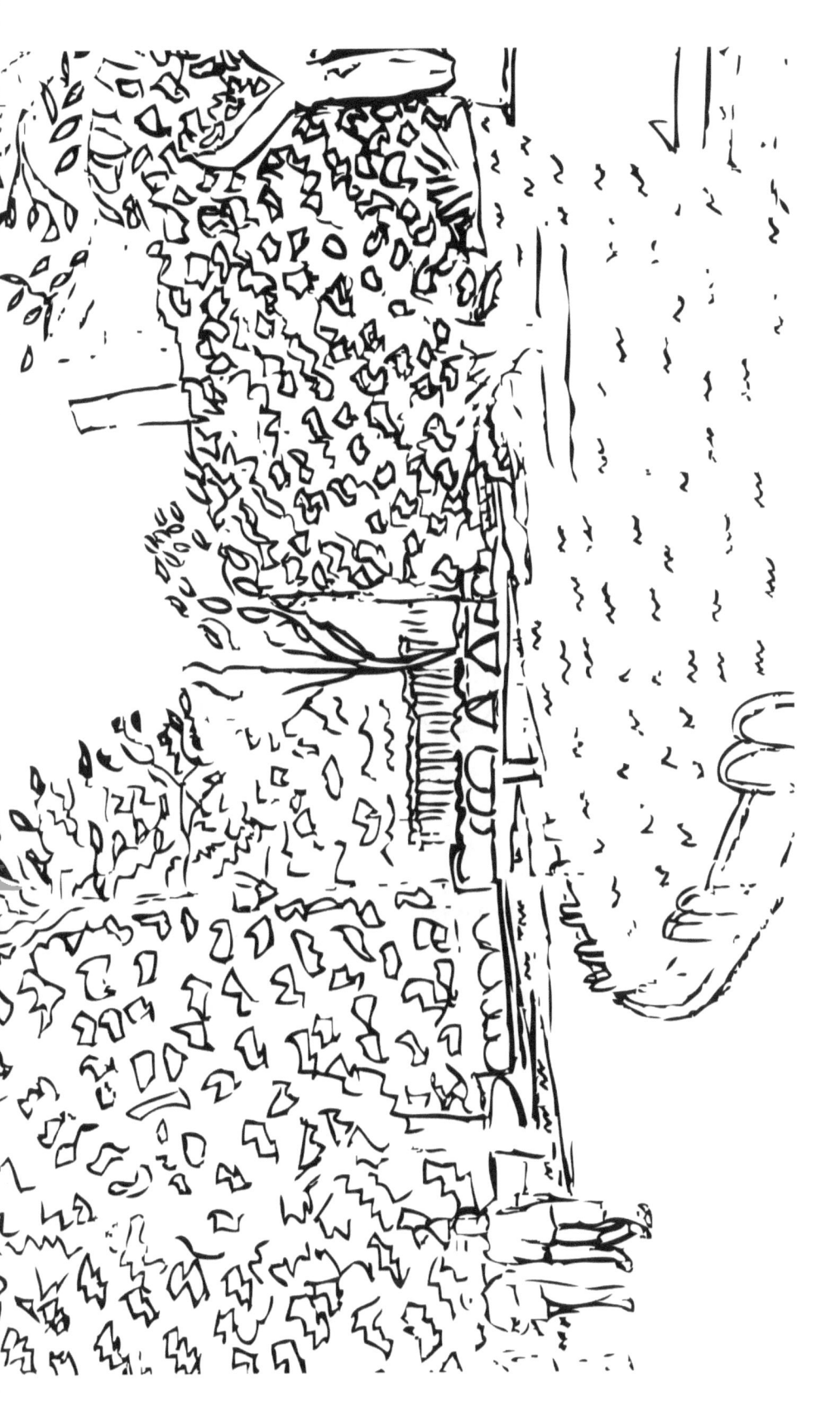

Color Scheme #1

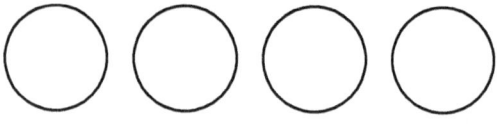

Color Scheme #2

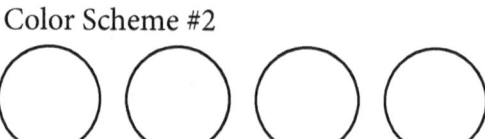

Color Scheme #3

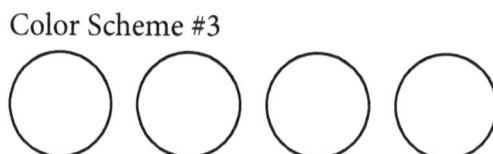

ABOUT THE AUTHOR

Roxana Ramos is a dedicated and empowered paper artist based in Peru. She got her B.A. in Studio Arts from the University of Rochester with a Minor in Women Studies.

She is a highly accomplished and multifaceted professional, going from teaching Visual Fundamentals at Toulouse Lautrec Design Institute, to running her bookbindery and creative laboratory Lettra in Lima, Peru.

Roxana has given talks and workshops in the subject of paper arts around the world. She has also been selected to exhibit in International Art Biennials showing her works in Bulgaria, UK, France, and Taiwan.

She is addicted to books and stationary, and loves traveling around the world sharing her love for the arts.

www.ingramcontent.com/pod-product-compliance
Lightning Source LLC
Chambersburg PA
CBHW050526290526
45786CB00007B/2713